Shirley H. Fowler
2000

P9-CQZ-112

MARY ENGELBREIT'S
HOME
COMPANION

Leading
the
Artful
Life

MARY ENGELBREIT'S
HOME
COMPANION

Leading
the
Artful
Life

Interiors designed with artistic intuition

Text by Vitta Poplar

Andrews McMeel
Publishing

Kansas City

Leading the Artful Life copyright © 2000 by Mary Engelbreit Ink
Photographs copyright © 2000 Universal Engelbreit Cox

All rights reserved. No part of this book may be used or reproduced in any manner whatsoever without
written permission except in the case of reprints in the context of reviews. For information, write
Andrews McMeel Publishing, an Andrews McMeel Universal company,
4520 Main Street, Kansas City, Missouri 64111.
www.andrewsmcmeel.com
www.maryengelbreit.com

🔲, Mary Engelbreit, and Mary Engelbreit's Home Companion are
registered trademarks of Mary Engelbreit Enterprises, Inc.

Library of Congress Cataloging-in-Publication Data
Engelbreit, Mary.
    Leading the artful life : from the pages of Mary Engelbreit's home companion : interiors
designed with artistic intuition / text by Vitta Poplar.-- 1st ed.
        p. cm.
    ISBN 0-7407-0997-6 (hc.)
    1. Interior decoration. I. Poplar, Vitta. II. Mary Engelbreit's home companion. III.
Title.

NK2110.E63 2000
747--dc21

                                                                            00-038692

First Edition
10 9 8 7 6 5 4 3 2 1

MARY ENGELBREIT'S HOME COMPANION
Editor in Chief: Mary Engelbreit
Executive Editor: Barbara Elliott Martin
Art Director: Marcella Spanogle

Produced by SMALLWOOD & STEWART, INC., New York City

Printed in Great Britain by Butler & Tanner Ltd., Frome and London

ATTENTION: SCHOOLS AND BUSINESSES
Andrews McMeel books are available at quantity discounts with bulk purchase for educational,
business, or sales promotional use. For information, please write to: Special Sales Department,
Andrews McMeel Publishing, 4520 Main Street, Kansas City, Missouri 64111.

contents

introduction

I've always felt it would be a little boring for every house to look like a "Mary Engelbreit house." In fact, I've been known to experiment with a few styles myself. The chapters in this book pretty much document my own moods at one time or another. It might come as a surprise to even my closest friends, but I think there is definitely a traditionalist in me. I would have to be a "New Traditionalist," which is what Chapter One of this book is all about. I once took on the job of decorating a stately 1914 neo-Georgian home with fine antiques and classic colors (you'll see a glimpse on page 12). Which is not to say that the house was stuffy. In certain rooms, I really let loose with my natural tendencies toward whimsy, incorporating birdhouses in one room and a handpainted mural on the ceiling of my studio.

When my husband, Phil, and I moved on to our next house, we built it from scratch, hoping to stream-line our possessions. We were definitely aiming for the look you'll see in Chapter Five, "The Bare Necessities," but alas, my own love of STUFF eventually took over, making the house ultimately look more like a page out of Chapter Three, "Bohemian Rhapsody." I admire those who are able to live with less, but I'm quite happy mixing and matching and having a field day at the flea market.

I guess I'm best known for my use of color—and I'm not shy about it. That's the message we're trying to get across in Chapter Two, "Primarily Colors." It hardly matters what the trendsetters say about which colors are in or out this year. What does matter is that you stick to your guns and decorate following your instincts. I don't see how you could ever go wrong that way.

Same thing if you're a gardener or nature lover. Even if you live in the heart of the city, it's entirely appropriate to have your home blossom with framed seed packets or garden rakes hung on the wall if that's what you like. If so, you'll find that inspiration in Chapter Four, "Drawn from Nature."

We offer this book to give you an idea of the gamut of possible ideas, and now it's up to you to find your own style. Maybe you'll reinvent yourself a few times along the way—but that's just part of the fun. Happy decorating!

Mary Engelbreit

new traditionalists

Nowadays, even museums don't furnish historic rooms by the book, knowing

that in any age and era there's always been a comfortable mix—call it "period imperfect."

And so we take the elements of tradition and give them a new twist: homes

with all the comforts of the past, firmly rooted in the present.

CHAPTER ONE

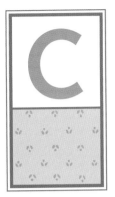

CERTAIN IMAGES COME TO MIND WHEN YOU hear the word *traditional*. Rooms swathed in fabric, strong color schemes like red and gold, opulent crystal accessories. When you decorate by adhering strictly to a period's rules, however, the results can be overwhelming. Rather, you'll want to suggest an era without strictly re-creating it.

There's no denying that English traditional style is one of the most popular of all to emulate. Few can resist the British love of comfort—their overstuffed feather and down furniture, rich woods, bird and botanical motifs, stitched samplers, Staffordshire dogs, and chintzware displayed in glass-fronted cabinets.

Yet the British are also champions of the eccentric. So feel free to throw a curve ball into the mix. Right in the middle of your traditional English drawing room outfitted with club chairs, tufted ottomans, a glistening chandelier, and plenty of sleeping dogs, invoke the spirit of the muse with an outrageous touch—be it a bowling-pin lamp or your old color guard uniform.

Instead of the usual portrait gallery of eminent ancestors, you could go so far as to display junk store portraits or paint-by-number landscapes that catch your fancy. You don't have a crystal chandelier? Substitute a bowl of crystals shimmering in a workaday kitchen bowl as a centerpiece.

The English passion for fabric allows you to mix and layer with abandon and never be "wrong." So if you adore batik, trust that it will go nicely with botanical pillows and Persian rugs. It just adds another layer to the visual richness.

Traditional doesn't always mean "formal." One of the most appealing Old World design schemes is that of the French country house. When re-creating it, think warm and sunny, since French country colors are traditionally vivid. Strong blues, earthy terra-cotta, sunflower yellow, and geranium pink glow softly on everything from woodwork to furniture.

OPPOSITE: **A hybrid of British and French styling, an Alabama guest house has graceful, lightweight furniture; a toile-covered cushion whispers of Provence.**
ABOVE: **Staffordshire cottages and castles bring an instant sense of Britannia to a California cottage. The pottery was made in large numbers in the 19th century and was often modeled after real structures.**

You needn't go on a trip abroad, however, to furnish a house in the French country spirit. Any accessories in the right color scheme would work, even if the objects would never be found in a French household. For instance, American Fiestaware could re-create the color scheme instantly. A collection of old classroom globes would add those needed touches of Mediterranean blue, while pinks could come from anything from a strawberry-hued old-fashioned wooden ice cream maker to a tricycle parked in the living room.

The French and English, and eventually all of Europe, joined forces, so to speak, in creating a Western style that sprang straight from the imagination. Chinoiserie, as the movement came to be known, has its roots in the 17th century, when Marco Polo brought back to Europe enticing tales of an exotic land called Cathay. People were smitten by the idea of a place so entirely different. Even today, in our global village, chinoiserie is as enduring as it is enchanting

BELOW LEFT: **In Mary's former Georgian-style home, her style took a more traditional turn—a Victorian firescreen is the proper hearth touch, but the lemon-colored twin McCoy topiary urns hint at a more playful spirit.** *BELOW AND OPPOSITE:* **Scrolls, umbrellas, and stylized flora on the fabrics used in both these rooms typify the motifs of chinoiserie, the Eastern look created by Western taste. In a graceful interpretation of the 18th-century French court's penchant for mixing styles, the homeowner has juxtaposed a Louis XVI-style settee with a Japanese folding screen.**

English cabbage roses and Asian-influenced floral fabrics harmonize so long as they share a color scheme.

LEFT: Toile de Jouy has triumphed over trends and still looks as fresh as when it first appeared in France in the late 18th century. Here the printed pattern takes the form of wallcovering in a Chicago conservatory. When using toile to create a French look, keep in mind that the results will be busy, so combine it with other fabrics in like colors, as this homeowner so wisely did with the ticking stripe on the armchairs. The energetic designs of toile also go a long way to camouflaging a room's architectural flaws. *ABOVE:* In the entry hall of Mary's townhouse, a gold "jester" table adds contemporary whimsy, while the vintage pink loveseat pays tribute to a lady's chamber of the past. At first glance, the stairway banister resembles exactly the sort found in grand old American homes, but look again and you'll notice the cherry-shaped cutouts—Mary's way of adding personality to even the most utilitarian structural areas.

LEFT: The sofa and armchairs are new, but the living room still has an Old World look. The secret is in the accessories—a Victorian cruet set on the table, Staffordshire dogs by the hearth, antique French needle-work over the mantel. Small touches like these make for a sum greater than the parts. OPPOSITE TOP: Ancestral portraits (whether genuine or not) are a surefire way of creating a been-here-for-generations look. The full set of Herend porcelain on the table was collected bit by bit. OPPOSITE BOTTOM LEFT: Positioned in a corner rather than centered as usual over a mantel or table, a 1913 portrait of a mother and child takes on fresh energy. White upholstery brings a contemporary look to the familiar wing chair shape. OPPOSITE BOTTOM RIGHT: The owners of this brand-new Chicago house gave it a retro feel by tiling the hearth in blue-and-white checks and filling its rooms with overstuffed English-style furniture.

BY THE 18TH CENTURY, CHINOISERIE WAS EVERYWHERE. NOT just porcelain but furniture, silver, and textiles sported branches of flowering fruits, fretwork, and jagged landscapes. Not only were such designs being made in the West, but they were also being made in China and India specifically for the Western market, with motifs that had never seen the inside of a pagoda. The style endured into ensuing centuries and continues even to the present—in the form of Blue Willow china, as an example. Its strength lies in its flexibility. For instance, just as Isabella, Marchioness of Hertford, added interest to her 1828 drawing room by embellishing hand-painted panels of fanciful Chinese scenes with cutouts from Audubon's "Birds of America"—not to mention French furniture and mirrors—you could use Asian motifs in as great or small proportions as you choose.

Keep in mind, it's your version of Asian, in the way American Chinese food re-invented authentic Chinese cuisine. What does it matter as long as you love it?

PATTERN tip

To update the patterned-all-over look, use a neutral shade for walls and furniture; add spark with accessories.

new traditionalists 17

LEFT: Taking her cue from the pastel palette of the Adam brothers, the 18th-century team of Scottish classicists, designer Shea Lubecke outfitted a dining room in shades of Wedgwood jasperware. Creamware and majolica add to the sense of history.

ABOVE: A detail of a dining room chair with a harlequin-point slipcover shows four different layers of fabric. If created in the usual heavy brocade and velvet textiles of traditional interiors, the results could be heavy, but because these materials are light and their colors soft, the effect is nothing short of ethereal.

GETTING THAT LOOK:

SWAGGERING CURTAINS

Formal interiors often incorporate lush window treatments. But this one from Chicago designer Shea Lubecke creates the richness without the fuss.

How to make 'em:

1. THIS WINDOW TREATMENT combines three different fabrics. The background is a sheer organdy panel that extends from floor to ceiling. The two inter-twined poufed fabrics are a salmon-and-white striped seer-sucker and a green-and-white striped silk. The seersucker hangs halfway down both sides of the window (with extra length allowed for swagging). Measure the green silk so that it hangs either halfway down the length of the window on both sides or halfway down the length on one side and full-length on the other (see opposite page).

2. FIT A TENSION ROD to the inside of window frame and hang the hemmed organdy panel.

3. ON ANOTHER ROD directly over the window frame, swag a generous amount of seersucker.

4. ON ONE OR BOTH SIDES of the window, tie the silk to the seersucker in a poufy knot.

When the English style gets re-created in St. Louis, interesting spins on convention are bound to happen. This chintz upholstery would be right at home in a wood-paneled or wallpapered drawing room with windows dripping yards and yards of fabric. But here the walls are the color of fresh lemons, and slatted blinds invite the light.

NATURALLY, YOU DON'T HAVE TO COMMIT YOURSELF TO A STYLE. You can be a magpie and borrow traditional elements from here and there and mix them up to your heart's content. The key is to add a healthy dose of imagination.

Rather than take the purely formal-fancy route, throw in juxtapositions that transcend eras and style. A 19th-century French giltwood armoire doesn't require a room filled with antiques of the same provenance. Instead, it could be the focal point in a space that is otherwise filled with simple Shaker-style furniture. A classic decorating icon like a camelback sofa could benefit from an updated slipcover—maybe something in a cotton-candy color or a dusky lilac. You'll see traditional pieces in a new light if you use them where they don't necessarily "belong"—for instance, an upholstered armchair in the master bath.

REINTERPRET AND PUT YOUR OWN SPIN ON THE FUNCTION of antique pieces. A portable vintage picnic table could be pressed into service as a coffee table; a former dough box might become a side table; or a salvaged tin ceiling remnant might frame a mirror.

One of decorating's fundamental golden rules is "don't fight the house." But you might tease it a bit. If a building is very formal in nature—perhaps it has a stately neoclassical facade—there's nothing to stop you from adding a few examples of simple, utilitarian, even primitive-style furniture rather than the expected elegant Georgian and Regency antiques. Conversely, a humble cottage filled with a few fine pieces takes on unexpected drama.

Follow a more relaxed approach to architectural details and woodwork as well, "deformalizing" them. Strip a Classical Revival fireplace of paint, then seal and wax it for a natural look that undercuts its stuffiness. Rather than adding gold leaf to crown molding, as is traditional, paint it citrus yellow. Turn lofty vaulted ceilings into something less forbidding by covering them and the walls in tone-on-tone stripes. Underplay rich wainscoting and paneling by painting them lighter colors, even bright white.

You can also convey the flavor of a period without getting it exactly right. As an example, rather than the classic rich red of an English countryside house, go for raspberry-pink walls, accented by glossy white paint on the woodwork. What pulls it all together might be a collection of creamware clustered on the mantel, some old, some new—a neutral touch that is a beautiful, tangible link with the past.

Looking for a centerpiece for the coffee table? Old seltzer bottles and decanters clad in tarnished silver evoke a vintage tintype aura.

Mary's Miniature Philosophy

"Miniatures are a great decorating tool because they work in traditional interiors, but they're also just plain fun. I like to mix them up—formal with frivolous."

At Mary's house, the family silver isn't the usual teapot, sugar bowl, and creamer assortment. Instead, a tiny couch, a cluster of cherries, and a calling card holder are whimsical expressions of a formal material.

PREVIOUS PAGES:
A sun-filled kitchen gets all the decoration it needs from blue-and-white transferware with Oriental motifs, a favorite of collectors since it first appeared in the 18th century. LEFT: Though it looks like a model American kitchen from the 1920s, this cozy room is a recent creation from the ground up. For an instant retro look, the homeowners added bun feet to their kitchen appliances. Though the floor looks like inlaid marquetry, it's actually a faux-painted diamond pattern. In the cabinets, there's a casual mix of 19th-century Spode and contemporary pottery by Californian Duncan Todd. OPPOSITE TOP: Vintage sinks and stoves aren't just for show—many work just as well as the day they were built. OPPOSITE BOTTOM LEFT: You'll find copper pots in every European chef's batterie de cuisine. These vintage examples have the names of their original owners stamped on the bottoms. OPPOSITE BOTTOM RIGHT: Kitchen-related collectibles like old cookie molds, vintage toasters, Bakelite-handled utensils, and cast-iron salesman's sample stoves (shown) are a natural for countertop displays.

IN WORKADAY ROOMS LIKE KITCHENS AND BATHS, 21ST-CENTURY technology is very much in evidence, so you need a good deal of ingenuity to get an old-fashioned look without affecting the practicality of the appliances.

Let's say you'd like French country in the kitchen. Hang copper pots from hooks or from an iron pot rack. Fill your pottery bowls with dried herbs, fresh lemons, your garden's latest bumper crop. Hang bulbs of garlic strung together. Arrange bottles of flavored oils and vinegars on countertops. Display your dishes on a plate rack. Spread Provençal-colored fabrics across your table. Paint the walls a warm umber.

Or go for Americana: Cut an antique screen door to fit the entrance to the pantry. Scout out a vintage stove. Reserve wall space for advertising signs and room on shelves for old advertising tins. In the bath, schoolhouse-style light fixtures will establish an Arts and Crafts mood. Create period appeal with white porcelain fixtures and nickel-plated fittings.

KITCHEN tip

Replace kitchen drawer pulls with old-fashioned ones from dressers and chests to create a "furnished" look.

new traditionalists 25

LEFT: In a bedroom that could easily be a case study for updated traditionalism, a tented canopy in a soothing shade revives the French art of the baldachin, or canopy bed, which customarily involves suspending a curtain from all sides to shut out drafts. In this scaled-down version using a miniature crown frame, the fabric extends only to the headboard, evoking a sumptuous air without the frou-frou. *ABOVE:* Never mind that this room is in the Midwest—it still exudes the elegant tranquility that makes a French boudoir so special. The center-piece is a *lit de repos*, or day bed, which became fashionable after the French Revolution. This particular example is double size, rather than the more common twin width. If you find an old daybed, don't despair if you can't find a mattress that fits, since "sized" beds as we know them are a 20th-century invention. Many mattress makers will custom-design one just for your antique bed.

Becky Portera

When Becky Portera and her husband, Louis, moved into their circa 1920 Dallas home in 1983, they owned nary a stick of furniture. This posed a bit of a problem, considering the house, being Georgian in style, is large and has ten-foot-high ceilings. "Every room was stark white. I started by painting the living room red, which made it look full and cozy even though there was nothing in there," recalls Becky, owner of Becky Portera Antiques. It was a trick she'd seen in pictures of English country houses, and to her amazement, it worked. Next she painted other rooms cream, to warm them a bit, and wallpapered the kitchen to "bring the ceiling down."

A needlepointer by avocation, Becky had always loved the cozy British sensibility, in which crewelwork, embroidery, and other hand-sewn touches are integral to the decorating scheme. So she decided to carry the theme throughout the house. But a

FAR LEFT: **The Porteras turned the family room's arched windows into French doors and added mahogany paneling for an old British library look.** *LEFT:* **Becky found the crown-shaped matchholder and striker in Scotland.**

new traditionalists 29

buying trip to England would have to wait. Red wing chairs, chosen to complement the living room's walls, were bought new from a local store, as was the blue leather sofa in the family room. "I knew that over the years it would age comfortably, thanks to my children."

Naturally, real British antiques did sneak in, like a pub bench that serves as a coffee table, a circa 1850 secretary, and a Gothic Revival child's chair. "Things from England didn't get really expensive until the late 1980s. I wasn't ahead of a trend, I just liked the style. It was easy to fill the house that way."

Eventually, Becky did take that trip abroad. And the happy tumble of barley twist candlesticks, needlepoint footstools, toby jugs, silver letter openers, and tiny brass tables all brighten her rooms. "I love the coziness of it all," says Becky. "I tend to move my collections around rather than ever part with any of them—you get so attached. There always seems to be room for more."

OPPOSITE: Becky purchased an 1856 Scottish print for thirty dollars. "Of course it would sell for a lot more money today, now that people recognize the true value of prints." *BELOW LEFT:* Becky's collections fill every inch. In a living room corner, a Georgian bowfront cabinet conceals, of all things, her plaster Santa Claus collection. Victorian needlepoint pictures—purchased before handiwork fever swept through auction houses— were part of her original inexpensive solution for filling the walls. Tortoiseshell boxes, all found in England, gather on the table in the foreground. *BELOW RIGHT:* Brass frames bring visual unity to a tabletop photo gallery.

MANORLY tip

The British always "finish things off": hang a painting by a ribbon, trim a lampshade with fringe.

BELOW: At the Porteras' Gulf Coast beach house, tradition takes a back seat but is still evident in little touches, like the 19th-century nautical-themed English transferware on display in the kitchen. ABOVE: Over the years, Becky has amassed a sizable stash of English and America bone cutlery from the late 1800s through the turn of the 20th century. "When I first started buying them, people thought it was strange, but now they're hard to find—and much too precious to put in the dishwasher. We do actually use them." RIGHT: "I've always loved the blue-and-white color combination, and when I discovered Blue Willow china years ago, that set me off in a new direction," says Becky. In her Dallas kitchen, even her curtains sport the centuries-old pattern.

primarily colors

Color comes prepackaged: Just look at a rainbow and see for yourself.

It's right there, organized and always the same. So why all the fuss? Enter the domain

of tints and tones and stay awhile. You'll not only learn a few things about the

world around you, but also about yourself.

CHAPTER TWO

AT THE HEART OF DECORATING IS THE COLOR scheme, but even to professionals color can be intimidating. When faced with an entire house, you need to make myriad decisions not only about the color treatment in each room, but about how it should vary from one room to the next.

Some people handle color with confidence. You'll find them quoted right and left, telling you that licorice black goes with candy-cane pink—but only in the dining room; every bedroom should be a whispery pale monotone. No one calls their bluff because no one's really sure of the "rules." Not only does color go in a direction around a wheel, but it can change from light to dark. Knowing which light goes with which dark can be a complex process. The result is that people either avoid mixing light and dark or are unhappy with their choices.

From a technical standpoint, there are primary colors—red, yellow, and blue— which, when mixed in different ways, give us secondary colors—orange (red and yellow), violet (red and blue), and green (blue and yellow). Mix the primaries with the secondaries, and you get shades like yellow-orange or blue-green. A smidgen of white pastelizes them, while a bit of black gives a deeper tone.

When you look at a color wheel, you can instantly see one color's relationship to others: complementary if it's directly across, analogous if it's adjacent, triadic if equidistant. By using a color wheel, you can feel confident, because you have a guide that tells what goes together, and it's indisputably true.

But what if, knowing you have this guide, you were to just forget about it for a moment. Who's to say which is more beautiful? Ask yourself—not the wheel—what colors you're drawn to, in which combinations. Why do those colors appeal to you? How much do they appeal to you? Even if you're passionate about purple you may not want to surround yourself with four violet-colored walls, but two fat grape-colored throw pillows could be just the right touch.

OPPOSITE: Color can be most cooperative. In this case, yellow, blue, orange, and red fairly dance against a neutral backdrop. The secret is that the hues are evenly distributed— from the folding chairs to the pail paintings by artist Toby Schachman.
ABOVE: The appealing periwinkle color on the wall was hardly a random choice: It was inspired by the owner's collections of enamelware, flowerpots, and plates—all of them blue.

primarily colors 37

BELOW: It doesn't hit you over the head, but this room's theme is decidedly blue and green (analogous colors). Green is more prevalent than you think—it's on the carpet, the book-bindings, and even the pillows.

ABOVE: Yellow on yellow? Why not, especially if it makes you happy. The color's reputation for jump-starting the brain is reason enough to use it liberally.

RIGHT: Blue and white is a fine pair, but it may need something to kick up the palette a bit—like this green weathered country corner cupboard. This tried-and-true palette is guaranteed to create a laid-back atmosphere in any room.

IF YOU REALLY WANT TO EXPERIMENT WITH COLOR, IT'S TIME to get out of the comfort zone and move forward. You've got to be willing to play—but there's no pressure, you don't have to "get inspired." Just be on the lookout for colors that please. It's your responsibility to find what you like. Pull pages from magazines. Save swatches of fabric, the lid of a Japanese tea tin, the pompom from a forgotten old lampshade. Visit a Buddhist temple and study the murals. These are the raw ingredients of experimentation.

Now that you've narrowed your color field, when you go shopping at flea markets you can zero in on those categories—making it infinitely easier to pick through the rows and rows of stuff and find what you're looking for. As a result of trusting your instincts, choosing paint colors won't be the daunting task that it's rumored to be. Tell yourself, as you slather a sunset hue on your living room walls or paint your floor the color of grass, you can always change things around later.

BELOW LEFT: **To find her perfect palette, artist Jeanine Guncheon dips into her subconscious and draws from her travels to South America.**
BELOW: **Color comes to the rescue in the form of pottery on an otherwise brown-and-beige porch.**
OPPOSITE: **When painter Linda CarterHolman creates a canvas, it's no holds barred on pattern and pigment. Like her artwork, her home is a tapestry of hues, lush as tropical fruit.**

Subtle colors in high-gloss paint have the same dramatic impact as bright colors in flat paint.

PAINTERLY tip

THERE'S A WHOLE VOCABULARY OF COLOR: VIBRANT, SOOTHING, provocative, racy. And there can be little doubt that color has an effect on our moods. What an incredible tool to have at your disposal: something that, by its mere appearance, will influence how you feel. When you pick a color and let everything revolve around it, you'll heighten that effect. So let's take a spin through the color world and see how you can use it to brighten, mellow out, or intellectualize your day.

Red brings warmth and excitement. It's a cheerful color that seems especially at home in living rooms, dining rooms, kitchens, and family rooms—places where people gather. The reason is that deep colors tend to approach us, which makes a room feel more intimate. If you live in a cold climate, red might just be your ticket to a cozy home. In your dining room, paint burgundy or claret on the walls. On the sunporch, coral-colored walls strike a more tropical note, while the color of brick in the home office brings a sense of purpose and order. A dose of tomato red will always wake up a staid kitchen; fill out the scheme with a 1940s Formica table with a gray-and-ketchup-hued "wave" pattern along the top, with matching chairs. And in the foyer, an unexpected dose of crimson walls finished with stenciled metallic gold stars can make even this unassuming space the most memorable in the house.

Everyone loves blue—it is all around us, in both the sky and the sea. The opposite of red, blue appears to recede, which is why it's so often chosen to "open up" a small room. But don't pigeonhole it based on this attribute: Blue in all its shades has a place everywhere. Paint your bedroom an Empire blue you once saw in a Paris

OPPOSITE: **Red has always been a popular dining room color because it's said to stimulate the appetite. Here, it's tweaked a notch and takes on a more lighthearted identity as raspberry pink.**

museum. Transform a dreary library with vibrant bachelor's-button blue, then decorate it with cobalt bottles and inkwells the color of lapis lazuli. Or surprise the blue color with something completely unexpected, like a fuschia kimono. Warm it all up with a yellow checkerboard floor.

Engelbreit Enlightenment

"If I stopped to consult a color guide every time I decorated, I'd be too confused even to buy a throw pillow. My method is simple: Please yourself."

In Mary's breakfast nook, cheerful checks are enough of an eye-opener that you can cut back on the coffee. To give the red-and-white checks some breathing space, she used plenty of florals and stripes.

PREVIOUS PAGES: Instead of a more conventional dining room shade, designer Jane Keltner painted her walls kumquat color. Since shades of orange have a similar impact to those of red, they are a pleasing substitute. *LEFT:* When you decorate with bold splashes of patterned color, as with this brilliant blue Talavera tile, rooms need little more in the way of adornment. *ABOVE:* Once a dull all-white space, this narrow kitchen got a fresh start with nothing more than paint and imagination. The sponged walls were inspired by that mellow orange shade found in Mediterranean textiles, while the cabinets are a hybrid of greens. To create their instant timeworn look, California artist Layson Fox used a crackle finish, available in kit form.

ARE YOU ENVIOUS OF THE WAY SOME PEOPLE JUST HAVE A WAY with green? More so than any other color, green has the ability to blend in with whatever's around it. Just gather up a basketful of greens—olive, sage, lime, leaf, and lichen—and set about giving them expression in your rooms. Let the celadon-soft tones of McCoy pottery contrast with a screen fashioned from weathered pistachio shutters. Set a parrot-green birdhouse alongside a bucket the color of pine boughs.

Yellow is rumored to be the most challenging color to the eye, but when you look at a room painted in buttery shades of straw and daffodils, that hardly seems possible. We're willing to believe that yellows stimulate mental powers; primrose-colored curtains and yolk-bright pillows seem to transport you to another place.

If you want a little romance, think violet—a feminine hue, to be sure. You don't need to paint the walls violet. Instead, hang a series of plates with orchid-hued borders and toss a lavender throw over a chair back.

BELOW LEFT: **One thick with butter yellow, the other doused in red, David Walker's monoprints bring color play to a breakfast nook.** *BELOW:* **In a Seattle potting shed, overcast days are brightened by fire-engine red and dandelion yellow.** *OPPOSITE:* **Black and white tile is a standard feature in vintage kitchens, but you can brighten it up with accessories that pop— 1940s fruit-themed wall hangings, pottery, and even a few floating fruits painted freehand on the wall.**

Prop painted sample swatches in strategic spots to see how the colors change with the light.

LEFT: In an Ohio home where artists live and work, an exuberant painting sets the mood for the family room. Blue ripples off the canvas onto a blanket chest, which serves as a table, as well as onto the china it displays. Hints of green find three-dimensional expression in the pottery and books on the coffee table, while the painting's rich scarlet strokes resonate in the homemade lamp's Warhol-esque tin-can base.

ABOVE: The best way to learn about color is by mixing it up yourself. You might even achieve your own "signature shade," which could be replicated at the paint store. Save your sample doodles. Keep a small lidded jar of custom paint handy to repair smudges so that you don't have to re-create the formula later on.

GETTING THAT LOOK:

STILL-LIFE SECRETS

"Composing a group of objects is like painting to me," says Roberta Williamson. Every corner presents an opportunity for a new work in progress.

How to do it:

1. SELECT YOUR BACKDROP. Blue is a recessive color suggestive of infinity, so blue-and-white china is an ideal choice.

2. BEGIN BUILDING your arrangement. Start at the center and work outward. Placed in the middle, and at the highest point, a clear glass vase adds a neutral layer of reflection. The beaded flower in yellow adds a lively complementary note. The nubbly texture of the beading provides a pleasing contrast to the smoothness of the china.

3. WHICH COLOR is exactly located between blue and yellow? Why, green of course! So frog, tree, and people figurines sporting this hue fill out the scene for a pleasing full spectrum look.

4. BY NO MEANS LIMIT yourself to figurines. Create your own tableaux with tiny buildings from an old railroad set, McCoy mixing bowls filled with odds and ends, dollhouse furniture, or tin toys.

LEFT: Since you start and finish your day with a visit to the bath, shouldn't its colors reflect something of who you are? Rather than going for an all-neutral scheme to create a tranquil look, the owners of a California bath outfitted it with a patchwork palette of tiles—every bit as soothing as white but much more interesting.

ABOVE: The color scheme for Mary Engelbreit's guest bath began with the diamond-check canary-yellow wallpaper. After that, says Mary, the rest fell easily into place. "I just gathered up anything yellow and it found a home in there." The inventory includes a chick planter, ducky jar (both great for holding toiletries), as well as several McCoy urns.

Jill Schwartz & Ron Ronan

Whether she's shopping the 26th Street flea market in Manhattan, strolling the aisles of the grand Brimfield antiques fair held three times a year in Massachusetts, or browsing in a French bazaar, designer Jill Schwartz is not just looking for that unusual piece—she's seeking inspiration for her home accessories company, Elements.

"It's all about collage," says Jill. "It's about taking as much different stuff as I could possibly think of and putting it together in an unusual way." The same principle that guides Jill to creating designs ranging from frames and photo albums to jewelry and paperweights also works in decorating her 1805 house in the Berkshire Mountains of Massachusetts, which she shares with her painter husband, Ron Ronan, and two young sons, Wyatt and Cooper. "I'm not into the way decorators work—limiting colors and designing down to the last tassel.

FAR LEFT: Only tiny (but noticeable) flares of color flicker in the neutral living room—for instance, sap buckets on a bracket shelf. *NEAR LEFT:* A toddler's clothes hanger marked Cooper, one of Jill's sons, becomes a nameplate to grace his bedroom door.

primarily colors 55

LEFT: Red lunchboxes are a leitmotif throughout the house. The frames, with their subdued, antiqued colors (courtesy of Ron Ronan) and vintage-button detailing, are Elements originals. *ABOVE:* Faded to brick, a tipsy old fire bucket serves as a flower container. *OPPOSITE TOP:* "I always add just a touch of color to my little vignettes," says Jill. In the dining room, the bingo card in just the right faded tomato shade gives the entire display a needed focal point. *OPPOSITE BOTTOM LEFT:* Without the tulip notecard in the background, the tiny flecks of red in the decades-old tape measure would be lost. *OPPOSITE BOTTOM RIGHT:* By virtue of their color, child-size club chairs—acquired separately—define Cooper and Wyatt's private area in the family room.

Instead, I tend to give a room a neutral backdrop, which is very freeing because everything works with it. Then I pick up what I like and it goes into the mix—the collage. Without realizing it, you begin to work around certain colors."

While Jill insists she's "not into bright," her favorite color is red. "It can be rich *and* subdued," she asserts. "Red has a really nice feel and does interesting things—it can work with colors that are more saturated or rather mellow. There's a smattering of red in every room of my house. It might be brought in with a pillow or artifact, or it could just be the smile on a stuffed animal. Or maybe only in a photo, in the carpet, or a lunchbox, or in a red metal rooster on a player piano."

Which is not to say that other colors don't surface. "Green is my other favorite—but not bright green like hunter. And shades of blue—never royal, but robin's egg, cornflower. I love the tints that are a little harder to come by, a little softer and rare—that's how you give a room intrigue."

Rather than assigning each room its own palette, pick a single color and weave it throughout the house.

primarily colors 57

BELOW: "I came across these children's gardening tools bundled together at a flea market," says Jill. "Their colors were irresistible." The subtle, mottled hues of their container, an old barrel, and nearby cookie tin provide contrast that let the tools stand out.

ABOVE: Originally, the European child's trundle bed in Cooper's room was a pale blue. But Ron wanted to give it more presence, so he played with paints to arrive at a soft antique green—though he left the carved star on the headboard its earlier color. "You have to be willing to experiment and be ready to squirt in another tint to get the color as close to your original idea as possible," he says. *RIGHT:* In Wyatt's headquarters, Ron pickled the pine walls as a subtle backdrop for color. Jill eschewed the usual child's fare for quirkier finds that contribute bursts of red and blue: a wall-mounted spring-loaded vintage game decorated with stars, a potato chip barrel that acts as a hamper, and an old store display to hold storybooks.

bohemian rhapsody

If you're drawn to the improbable harmony between an ancient basket and a
modern wire chair, the sheer exuberance of a homemade shell-covered vase juxtaposed
with a carved Appalachian cat, then chances are good you threw away the
decorating rule book eons ago. Let your natural sense of whimsy create your private utopia.

CHAPTER THREE

WHEN YOU DECORATE TO REFLECT WHO YOU ARE, naturally the first thing you must come to terms with is, what do you really like? Don't hold back. Be honest. Yes, you really do covet those nodding dogs and pagoda lamps you remember from your aunt's living room. You once paid good money for 1950s homemade "pebble pictures" at a yard sale. You see nothing untoward in bringing children's sandbox toys indoors and featuring them as a centerpiece. Or maybe the 1960s are truly your era—even if you weren't born yet. Silk-screened wall coverings, tie-dyed pillows, beadwork, and other totems of the period are still out there in secondhand stores, ripe for a new counterculture.

It sometimes takes daring to come to terms with your true style, but once you do, life gets so much easier. You no longer have to worry about "matching" anything. If you're confounded by those quizzes in magazines that beckon you to "find your decorating style," take heart: You're not alone, and you certainly don't have a split personality. Most of us aren't so easily classifiable—for instance, having a "country look" or "glamorous style." For the most part, we like to mix it up.

Follow your bliss and let your ruling passion be your muse. Rooms don't have to be labeled or serve a specific function. Are you a "chair person?" Then populate a room only with wonderful whimsical chairs in any period or style, from child size to grown-up—perhaps the quirky creations of a 1940s *artiste* whose backs are in the shape of suites of the playing card deck. Do you love ballet? Turn a bath into a virtual ballet studio, complete with shimmering scrimlike curtains, a ballet barre towel rack, figurines, and music boxes that play "Stardust."

You're no longer bound by convention, so why not create twists on the expected? In the dining room, for instance, instead of the classic sideboard or china hutch, create your own *cabinet de merveilles* or *wunderkammer*—actually, a 17th-century practice of wealthy barons, who would fill their cupboards with oddities and

OPPOSITE: **Sometimes, seemingly useless items suggest the cleverest decorating ideas. Here, Texas designer Carol Bolton dangled a bunch of forgotten keys and old house numbers from a chandelier. Never mind that the light doesn't work!** *ABOVE:* **Seattle milliner Cheri Ellis painted the Oriental motifs on the wooden boxes in her studio by hand, though you could get the same exotic effect using craft glue and Asian fabrics.**

bohemian rhapsody 63

curiosities. Yours might be a clinical-looking metal cabinet, the kind favored by school nurses for dispensing cotton balls and gauze—filled with kewpie dolls displayed alongside an antique medical model and a circa 1920 hood ornament. In other words, anything you like.

Think of your home as an ever-changing stage set; that way, you're free to experiment and even go a little overboard, safe in the knowledge that you can always change it around later. Decorating is as much about subtracting as adding—so have the courage to edit what you own. At the same time, if you feel a room lacks a certain "something," you don't always have to run out and spend money to get it. The thrill of discovery that so many collectors wax poetic about doesn't necessarily mean traipsing all over the country. What you need may already be right there under your nose—stuffed in the closet or lurking in the basement or hibernating in the garage. It just needs you to bring it to light.

BELOW LEFT: **Before casting aside furniture, consider creative rehabilitation. Decoupaged with sheet music, a once bland side chair is now singing a new tune.** *BELOW:* **A figurative model mingles with porcelain knickknacks. The contrast between folksy and refined elements is what gives the grouping its verve.** *OPPOSITE:* **Those necklaces—didn't they come from an island paradise? Is that a shopping list from 1973 hanging on the opposite cupboard door? The memories of one collector's life form a three-dimensional album, from a school lunch box (bottom shelf) to a mini watering can bought at a garden gift shop (top shelf) to the number of her high school locker (in penholder).**

BROWSING tip

When strolling the flea market, look for furniture with good bones; you can always change the finish later.

ABOVE: It's not the same old drill for this Deco dental cabinet—it now displays vintage barware and table accessories—which just goes to show that you should never let an object's original function govern its use today. Forget what room a piece was designed for. One of the freeing aspects of decorating is to toss out preconceptions.

RIGHT: Do you ever get the feeling that you're being watched? This Chicagoan's collection of doll and mannequin heads gazes out wistfully from a far corner. But there's so much more to see! Aside from the old railway station lounge furniture reupholstered in an abstract 1960s print, there's the sculpture at its side—a welded-

together assemblage of broken outer-space toys perched on tomato-juice-can legs. Just to throw you off the scent of being able to categorize the mix as "eclectic 20th century," the fluted lines of a neoclassical column in the corner give the room a whiff of antiquity as it continues the linear feeling of the window blinds.

LEFT: Schoolbook characters take a south-of-the-border vacation in graphic artist Bianca Juarez's hybrid-style home office. What unites it all is a strong color quotient and sense of fun. For those months when her fireplace isn't in use, Bianca fills it with sock monkeys, board games, and tin toys.

ABOVE: The next time you need a new desk accessory, resist the urge to run to the office supply store. It will definitely not stock such treasures as vintage snuff boxes from Sweden, as seen here. You can also bet that the store won't have a "Tunisian sea grass and bamboo chair" section.

FOLLOWING PAGES: Your office needn't be all work and no play. Take the lead of illustrator Lane Smith— frame an Etch-A-Sketch, display a train ticket to Peoria or a haircolor ad from the 1950s. Inspirational "walls of wonder" like this are an important artist's tool for creativity.

LEFT: Think beyond the literal, and where others see trash, you'll spot possibilities. In this case, a window grate became a pot rack—though a ladder, garden gate, or child's Flexible Flyer sled could do as well. *OPPOSITE TOP:* Chandeliers are made for embellishment—hang your own beads and baubles on a pre-existing model. *OPPOSITE BOTTOM LEFT:* Forget about exact matches. Rugs from Turkey mix easily with throws and pillows from Mexico and the Southwest. *OPPOSITE BOTTOM RIGHT:* Painter Jeanine Guncheon found Spanish tiles fifteen years before she installed them on her kitchen backsplash.

WHEN YOU COMMIT TO BOHEMIAN WAYS, SOMETIMES THE LACK
of guidance can be as disconcerting as the rules themselves. If you'd like a bit of
structure, consider this: Some mystics begin their days by hurling a copy of the
I Ching (or Book of Changes) to the floor to see what message it opens to. This is as
good a technique as any for your decorative schemes. For example, the words
"Abundance has success" or "One should strive to attain small things only" could be
helpful guides for shopping a flea market on a Saturday morning.

Another possible tactic is to borrow a tip from short-story writers and take five
disparate "scenes"—or objects—and randomly splice them together. Now you've
got a tale to tell. A saxophone lounges on the mantel next to a lady-head vase.
Chinese jars are filled with Asian paintbrushes and tiny whisk brooms. Once you start
creating tableaux of the subconscious, they tend to multiply, as friends show up on
our doorstep with miniature railway benches and 1920s dog bowls.

MOVABLE
tip

*You can never have enough trays: they make it
easy to move your collections around.*

bohemian rhapsody 73

Though designed as a floorcloth, this serene angel by Chicago artist Karen Morava is beautiful enough to elevate to the role of art on the wall beyond a pencil post bed. The cross came from a Mexican flea market; the African blanket on the trunk at the foot of the bed is made from hair and wool.

ADMIT IT, YOU HAVE A GYPSY SOUL. OFTEN, OUR BEST MEMORIES are travel-related. That summer in Europe just after college—you still have the plates you bought at the Paris flea market. Years later, on business, you fell in love with the East—the temples, with their incredible flower creations, and all those handmade textiles flapping in the breeze in vendors' stalls. Who could resist?

It's a downright shame to put such keepsakes in a drawer. Instead, bring those mementos into the light, and let them mix freely with the flotsam and jetsam of your life, be it family photos, fine antiques, decorative bric-a-brac or junk-shop gems. Then there's life's voyage. Little things mean a lot: your child's first report card, a pocket watch you received on your 30th birthday, your grandmother's old pendant. What would happen if they came together on a tabletop?

GETTING THAT LOOK:

SEEING BEYOND THE OBVIOUS

Okay, so this isn't exactly a "project." It's more of an adventure, an exercise in imagination that you can easily accomplish on a Saturday morning.

How to search for treasure:

1. HEAD TO A FLEA MARKET with a limited amount of money and the goal of finding the "perfect thing."

2. YOU HAVE NO IDEA WHAT the perfect thing is. Remember, you're going with an open mind and a curious eye.

3. FIRST TAKE A GRAND TOUR of the aisles in a quick sweep, then go back to peruse the possibilities. On your first trip through, don't cut across aisles, or you'll miss half the booths. Make notes; carry a tape measure; jot down locations; use a Polaroid camera to record items.

4. MAKE YOUR SELECTION(S): You could use that washtub as a planter, but turn it upside down, put a piece of glass on top, and you have yourself a coffee table. And, yes, the Radio Flyer scooter, above, would look just right in a living room display with old toys.

BELOW: In a bedroom, vintage Christmas lights became an above-bed mural. Circa 1970s fabrics—once scorned by those guardians of "good taste"—turn the bed into a bevy of memories. The canopy is simply pink gauze primped with faux flowers. Perfection!

ABOVE: On the opposite side of the same room, the owner dressed up a thrift-store mirror by screwing in cup hooks to display her key tag collection. A swag of sunglasses hangs above.

RIGHT: At first glance, we see stately classical globes as part of the frame of an antique bed. But look again and the scene changes—the globes are really stone balls from an old French lacrosse-like sport, balanced on their game sticks, which are now bedposts.

TO GIVE YOUR COLLECTIONS NEW OOMPH, BRAINSTORM NOVEL ways to show them off. Jewelry, for instance, is every woman's quandary. If you have drawers overflowing with old rings and bracelets—many in disrepair—just empty their contents into a collection of 1950s clutch purses and show them off on a vanity.

St. Louis illustrator Pat Brangle rationalizes it this way: "Jewelry is an art form like anything else. I've always kept my collections on view." Her suggestions: Show off both necklaces and pins on dressed mannequins. Install a floor-to-ceiling pegboard painted in a dramatic color and hang jewelry from the pegs, in large-scale geometric patterns if you like. Or cover a bulletin board with black felt and pin jewelry to the felt.

Even the most humble collection takes on a certain flair when well displayed. For instance, on their own, ordinary key tags don't amount to much. But hang each one individually from a cup hook in a row along the wall, and now you've got something.

Set up a "creative friction" between objects by playing with contrasts: rough versus smooth, fine art with folk art. Dolls' heads might share shelf space with sculpture; flea market candlesticks shed a different light on heirloom crystal. Intriguing juxtapositions inspire double takes: a chalkware poodle with a French mercury-glass wigstand,

OPPOSITE: **"I tend to collect more jewelry than I could ever possibly wear," says Mary Engelbreit. The solution to her superfluity of necklaces was to show them off on an old display rack (think Woolworth's, circa 1965). Set up in front of a window, the collection catches the light. What's more, the necklaces don't get tangled together, and it's easy for Mary to choose which ones she would like to wear.**

maybe, or a wall display of old gameboards punctuated by a skateboard.

Find the charm in imperfection: the cracked clock face, the rusted garden chair. But don't be afraid to upgrade: Think of what creative applications of paint, gold leaf, and decorative hardware will do. Play around with antiquing and decoupage techniques. Dip photos in coffee or tea to "age" them. Change a room's mood instantly with a few pastel-colored paper lanterns. It's all completely up to you.

The Queen's Jewels

"In a way, jewelry boxes are silly. What on earth is the point of having all this great stuff if it never sees the light of day?"

ABOVE: **One joy of costume jewelry is showing it off at home. A vintage painted doll obligingly holds an assortment of trinkets strung round her neck.**

LEFT: No one of significance ever decreed that baths must be boring. So get out of the antiseptic white mode and have a fling in color and pattern. Since this bath opens directly into the master bedroom of artist Martha Young's Maine getaway home, it had to be as beautiful as the rest of the space. Set on a diagonal, the tilework brings a harlequin note of whimsy, heightened by the linen dressing gowns that decorate the room with a princess touch.

NEAR LEFT: Pepto Bismol pink is as fine a color as any for a medicine cabinet.
BELOW: In Wisconsin-based artist/designer Tracy Porter's bath, the door itself holds the key to the interior's tumult of color, from a hand-striped mirror to a skirted sink trimmed in fabric leaves.

Belinda & Jesika Hare

You could say an early sign that something different was afoot was when Belinda Hare, age eight, stitched her very first 4-H project—not the usual poncho or apron, but a modish bikini. While the judges might have raised an eyebrow or two, they had to admit—the girl's got talent!

And Belinda has been busily designing to please herself ever since. At Flashback, her Austin, Texas, shop, you'll find not just vintage clothing, but fabrics and furniture that reflect her own sense of style—not to mention that of her daughter and co-worker Jesika. "Her taste is more 1970s," says Belinda. "You know, mushroom lamps and sprays of revolving flowers that light up." But mother has never discouraged daughter from finding her own way.

Their home life reflects this mixed-bag approach. Fine pieces sit alongside what Belinda unhesitatingly terms "junk." Which is not to say she won't spend money

FAR LEFT: **"I've always loved hanging things from the ceiling and having *lots* of stuff to look at,"** says Belinda, whose bedroom bursts with Balinese parade umbrellas and painted velvet souvenir pillows. *LEFT:* **A pink velvet box is just a fraction of her "smalls" collection.**

bohemian rhapsody 83

LEFT: A poem enlarged to fit a frame and a clock that ponders the mysteries of infinity make a dramatic back-drop for the Hares' home files. The toy truck is Texas-size.

ABOVE: Mason jars and glass refrigerator containers serve as vitrines holding unlikely treasures.

OPPOSITE: "The coffee table in the living room is just junk, but when you apply fabric with upholstery nail heads to the top you've made it into a cute piece," say the Hares.

on a piece when she falls in love with it. In her living room, for instance, a 19th-century oil painting of a reclining nude—bought on a Northeast scavenging trip—presides over pieces of unknown provenance. But, Belinda is quick to point out, "I have lots of prints I love as much as paintings. To me it's not about the value of a piece. It's about loving it and having it speak to you, maybe bringing back a memory of someplace charming or romantic you've been."

Belinda can't pinpoint any one single influence. Yes, she caught the bug for using timeworn heirlooms while on buying trips in Europe. But she also happily decorates with plenty of Asian motifs—from Indonesian umbrellas to Chinese newspapers—though she's never actually visited the East. In fact, she feels that everything you need to know you can learn on your own home turf: "Texas is so diverse," says Belinda. "There's culture here, from the Fredericksburg Germans to the Mexican population and the Native Americans. That's why I'm here."

OPPOSITE: "Fabric hides a multitude of sins," says Belinda. "You can take the most ordinary things and dress them up. The lacy panels attached to this old hutch made it dreamy." *BELOW LEFT:* "I love making something out of the most inexpensive objects." Craft scissors turned Chinese newspaper into scallop-edge shelving. *BELOW RIGHT:* "I am a pack rat. Every single closet and drawer is full of stuff." That's why Belinda puts her collections to use whenever possible, turning a teacup into a tieback, for instance.

ARTISTIC tip

Swag curtain fabric from unusual holders like glass doorknobs and wooden spools.

bohemian rhapsody 87

drawn from nature

Do you dabble in daisies? Cater to cattails? Find a certain frisson in ferns?
Then you'd certainly revel in a home where nature comes indoors. When you surround
yourself with the earthy textures of leaf and twig and bark, fabrics with botanical motifs, and
outdoor objects put to charming use indoors, every day is a walk on the wild side.

CHAPTER FOUR

AT ONE TIME OR ANOTHER, WE ALL LONG TO GET away—perhaps to that cabin in the woods where the scent of pine smoke wafts from the chimney. It's the kind of place where you take a morning dip in a mountain lake, followed by a bit of trolling on the creek with lunch in a grove of shagbark hickories. Maybe that cabin will always be a dream. Or it's just a place that you get to only in summer. But there's a solution to your campfire cravings: Bring the cabin to you. Create a rustic retreat that celebrates nature in your own home.

You don't have to be a backwoods whittler to create an authentic sylvan style. It relies on a few time-honored touches. Any and all of the following will do: pine-cone motif plates, 19th-century brown-and-white transferware, flatware with bark-style celluloid handles, Adirondack and other rustic chairs, oil lamps, vintage balsam pillows printed with lakeside scenes, handcrafted walking sticks, miniature birch-bark canoes and tepees, and plenty of striped and checked Indian trade-type blankets.

Anything twiggy will fit in. Pruned branches and undercuttings can yield curtain rods, a tripod plant stand bound with rope and nailed together, even a simple wall rack for hanging caps and the dog's leash. If you get really ambitious you could try making a whole bed canopy from rustic twigs, or at least embellishing a preexisting structure by wrapping grapevines all around.

When you turn a single room into an angler's retreat, there's always a place you can dip into for peaceful moments. Sheathe the walls in birch bark, an atmospheric backdrop for vintage photographs of old fishing camps or feather, tinsel, and floss flies from your grandfather's tackle box mounted and framed under glass. On the mantel, display fly-tying reference books and anything with a fishing theme, spools of fishing line, a fishing net, even salmon-shaped salt and pepper shakers. Let a bamboo rod lean beside a Native American bark creel. And don't forget the pre-1930 wooden fishing lures—pile their colorful shapes like Swedish fish in a penny candy jar.

OPPOSITE: **An inherited turn-of-the-20th-century summer cabin became a full-time home for the grandchild of the original builder. Twig furniture and ticking pillows emphasize the rough-and-tumble atmosphere.**
ABOVE: **A bulletin board covered with moss and chicken wire becomes headquarters for botanical studies. Pin up planting schedules, seed labels, a list of butterfly-friendly plants— anything gardening-related.**

drawn from nature 91

BELOW: A trio of pith helmets and an insect identification chart suggest expeditions into the blue yonder in search of rare winged creatures. But the more refined transferware plate and framed botanical etchings tame the wilderness note for indoors. A collection of wicker-wrapped bottles nestled in a woven tray picks up the subtle weave of the settee.

ABOVE: The brilliant colors of butterflies set the color scheme for a nature corner. So long as the tones are in harmony, you can slip in anything whimsical you like, from a doll's chair to a vase.

RIGHT: Take an old frame and outfit it with a fine mesh, and you've got display space for anything from ladybug pendants to fishing tackle. The wire screen acts as a scrim that enhances the sense of age of the collectibles behind it. In the foreground, old garden pots gather, and antiquarian books are nice pedestals for miniatures.

LEFT: Old rakes emphasize the airy proportions of a San Francisco living room with French countryside overtones. OPPOSITE TOP: Before radio and television, the birdcage served as a family entertainment center. This openwork metal example cheerily echoes the canary yellow roman shades above. OPPOSITE BOTTOM LEFT: It looks like the ablutions room in a medieval Italian castle, but this guest bath is actually located in the heart of Los Angeles. The aura of antiquity comes from the carved stone wash basin, with the plumbing camouflaged by the pedestal below it. Sights like this are not as unusual as they once were, since designers are increasingly employing special effects like natural boulders as part of bath decor. OPPOSITE BOTTOM RIGHT: Write yourself a ticket to paradise and pot up zesty aromatic plants like thyme, rosemary, and scented geraniums, whose ruffled foliage is a visual treat in itself. Take a country drive and look for off-the-beaten-path nurseries with resident potters crafting unusual designs, like these scalloped-rim terra-cotta creations.

You might even find the outdoor touch you're looking for in your own basement—in the form of Scouting and camping gear. Set up a hallway table still life complete with official Scouting paraphernalia, from flashlights, canteens, and cups to cameras, whistles, and pinback buttons. Thermoses, telescopes, water-proof match boxes, and even a quartet of old tent pegs will all glow in the light of a camp lantern. Paper the interior of a cabinet with color copies of pre-1920s manual covers or a U.S. Geological Survey map that recalls your hiking exploits.

While you're at it, camp it up. In the early years of the 20th century, making quilts from old summer camp and school pennants—their felt letters appliqued on wool—was a popular craft. If you can't find one during your antiquing forays, make your own rug or patchwork bedspread from antique pennants. Just a single large pennant reading, "Camp Wekenokie" hanging from the top of a pine cupboard brings back memories of sleeping bags and toasted marshmallows.

Natural tip

To decorate a kitchen, use an old enameled kitchen colander lined with moss as a flower container.

drawn from nature 95

LEFT: Sometimes, the house itself suggests the decorating style. This columned sunporch is far too formal for a rustic look, so the owner went with a more traditional botanical print theme and painted her wicker white. An emerald green floor keeps this wickerwork wonderland from looking like it might float away.

ABOVE: Plant containers that hook over the top of cabinet doors, window-box style, make it possible to have a touch of greenery anywhere. If you want to add little bouquets to your walls, seek out old-fashioned wall pockets.

drawn from nature 97

"EARTH LAUGHS IN FLOWERS"

HERBS

LEFT: If there's an unused outbuilding on your property, consider turning it into a summer retreat. Clean out your closets of all those can't-find-a-use-for-them baskets and hang them as a decorative canopy. Have a field day with garden ornaments too fragile or inappropriate for the yard—for instance, a concrete frog or even a flock of flamingoes. As you make your annual springtime garage-sale pilgrimage, keep an eye open for possible inexpensive decor—for instance, straw hats for a quarter a piece become works of art when hung on the wall. *ABOVE:* Fill the corners of your summer retreat with whimsical displays—perhaps a pair of binoculars with an egg basket and dried hydrangeas.

GETTING **THAT** LOOK:

YOUR SEAT AWAITS...

Table cards for an alfresco wedding or other outdoor event needn't be the usual affair. Try these pressed flower designs at your next special occasion.

How to make 'em:

1. FILL A BASKET WITH FLOWERS and greens of assorted shapes and sizes: pansies, hydrangeas, daisies, roses, yarrow, borage, and ferns are good choices.

2. SLIP EACH FLOWER, PETAL, and leaf between the pages of a heavy book. Let them dry at least

three weeks in a cool, dark place, without moving the book.

3. WITH A PINCH OF CRAFT glue, arrange the flowers in "bouquets" on note cards. Don't try to make them identical, just similar in size. Glue a bow at the top of each arrangement.

4. WITH AN ARTIST'S BRUSH and watercolor paint, add the table number freehand. First draw out the numerals from 0 to 9 so the cards have a consistent look. Practice with watercolors on the same kind of paper until you achieve the effect you want.

NOT ONLY FLOWER CHILDREN WANT TO GET BACK TO THE garden. The botanical fresh-as-nature style appeals to everyone on some level, and you can adapt it to your home in ways both subtle and ambitious.

If you're new to decorating *au naturel*, there are small things you can do to get started before making a big commitment to the style. Simple touches include dangling herb bouquets from the rafters or showing off a collection of mason jars filled with seedpods on the mantel. Turn a potting bench into a sideboard for the sunroom. Let guests take a seat on overturned garden urns. Have an old-fashioned glass cloche show off a collection of vintage flower frogs (those spiky or cagelike anchors for flower arrangements). Group country treasures on a table: a bark bird-house, a pressed herb print, and a vase of sunflowers.

Speaking of sunflowers, because they dry so beautifully and have a long season (mid-July through early September), these gentle giants are a great way to decorate.

Display them in a tall glass vase filled with lemons and water; let a single head flop out of a teacup or float a couple of heads in water with tea candles for a dreamy centerpiece. Fresh sunflowers (tucked into florists' vials) make adorable accents to curtain tiebacks.

If you want a simple look, let botanical prints do all the decorating for you—for instance, prop up reproduction illustrations of heirloom cabbage roses by 19th-century French master Pierre-Joseph Redouté. Or if you hang them in a perfect grid in dime-store frames, the prints will create a graphic rhythm that makes a room seem airier.

OPPOSITE: **Chez Engelbreit, a sunny corner is outfitted in shades of green. Notice the abundance of ivy, which thrives with minimal care.** *ABOVE*: **Enamelware was painted freehand with acrylics and a fine-tipped brush.**

Mary's Bon Mots

"I don't have a green thumb so I fill my plant stand with collectibles instead. I still get that natural look, with no watering."

Catch the artificial flowers on Mary's plant stand? These days faux flowers and foliage can be quite convincing, and even the ones that are frankly fake have a certain charm.

BEFORE YOU CLEAN OUT THE TOOL SHED, TAKE A SECOND LOOK
at the decorative possibilities that lurk in the cobwebs. Old watering cans could be resurrected as vases for fresh flowers. Yesterday's sprinklers bring a note of sculpture to your curio cabinet—or use them as paperweights when you write letters on the porch.

For those who are dedicated leaf lovers, a more ambitious approach is clearly needed: create a total garden environment. One way is to turn a sun-starved room into an arcadia by painting it the colors of tropical leaves. Choose different shades of green and apply each one, gradually deeper, with a roller in a floor-to-ceiling stripe. No need to do any measuring, since the stripes' unevenness enhances the natural look. To fill the walls, hang pressed ferns in creamy white frames. Or try the same effect with a pink-to-raspberry palette, featuring rose prints as your decoration.

Another painted effect is to "grasscloth" the walls: roll on a soft green base color, let dry; then dip a dry paintbrush into a topcoat color—a deeper green or yellow—

OPPOSITE: One big sylvan surprise can make all the difference. In this case, a moss tablecloth edged in raffia brings a casual woodsy feel to an otherwise formal room. *BELOW LEFT:* More moss cascades from a lamp shade (courtesy of a glue gun). A wire shoe filled with rose petals and a candleholder balancing the cone of a lodgepole pinecone make for a fragrant, touchable tablescape. *BELOW RIGHT:* Are you an aspiring entomologist? Even if you don't know the difference between a swallowtail and a sawbeetle, you're free to collect framed glass-encased insects at auctions and antiques shops. To continue the theme in other corners of the room, display bee skeps, butterfly nets, and vintage microscopes.

POT LUCK
tip

Clay pots for orchids have lots of tiny holes on their sides, a perfect partner for a polka-dot scheme.

drawn from nature 103

brush off as much paint as you can on newspaper so there's barely any left on the brush, and apply a tic–tac–toe grid—top to bottom, left to right—in short strokes to get an authentic thatched look.

While you're still in a painting mode, let your favorite botanical image or flowered fabric be the inspiration for a scene painted freehand on a secondhand table, a screen, or shutters. Or base-paint a cupboard pale glen green, then use a glue stick to temporarily affix ferns to its doors; lightly spray-paint around the edges of the ferns with a slightly darker shade of green for a leafy stencil impression.

Plants can't flourish without sunlight. Turn curtains into a blooming garden. Using textile paints, stencil on botanical motifs—dandelions, poppies, peapods. Or have a copy shop make heat transfers of plant pictures you can iron onto cotton fabrics.

PREVIOUS PAGES: Animal prints and botanicals cozy up on a 19th-century daybed. The leaf portraits are actually the handiwork of decorator Suzedie Clement. "I gather parts of ferns, scented geraniums, lamb's ear, ivy, coralbells—which give the purple tones. Then I use craft glue to make them adhere." *ABOVE:* These Dutch bird-themed tiles can be used as trivets. *LEFT:* Botanical details on plates have been popular for centuries, but nothing surpasses majolica for realism and whimsy combined. Majolica earthenware, glazed in bright hues in high or low relief, has been popular since the 19th century. *OPPOSITE:* Nature glides into the kitchen with a few imaginative touches: Ivy trails around a transfer-ware teacup, while a trio of bird prints chirp over the sink.

106   leading the artful life

BELOW : Distressed-finish furniture is a natural for the garden look. Its timeworn surfaces suggest a rural lifestyle. Though this bedroom has a restrained pastel palette, note the color of the French doors, just peeking out of the corner of the picture. Their hue provides a graceful transition to the flower-filled patio.

ABOVE : Clearly, a gardener lives here. The clues are blowsy floral print fabric, streaming sun, and a mug of cut flowers.

OPPOSITE : With windows thrown open, indoors and out are as one in a California bedroom. A throw tossed on the bed and other green touches provide a visual stepping-stone to the leafy treetops outdoors. Tied on simply with fabric bows, the bed's canopy can be changed at a moment's notice: mosquito netting in summer or warm pastels in winter.

AN ARTFUL LIFE:

Karen Dominguez-Brann

A landscape of 1,132 wind-swept acres in the Santa Monica mountains is a tough act to follow. But Karen Dominguez-Brann has her ways. The owner of Foxglove Design and a part-time painter, she has created a homestead amid this wild paradise that is every bit as breathtaking as its surroundings.

"Colors should be a continuum," believes Karen, who designs gardens all along the California coast. "So from the inside looking out it feels like the same space—the outside comes inside and vice versa. To tell if you're making the transition correctly, just take a photo. When your eyes look at something, you don't 'see' everything. But a camera tells the truth."

While the garden immediately surrounding her 1880s Craftsman-style home has been tamed with roses, grapes, wisteria, and hollyhocks, the interior is filled with botanical textiles in the same motifs and colors. And it's little wonder: Karen thinks

FAR LEFT: Outdoors as in, Karen picks a color—in this case, purple—and bases everything on it, from the periwinkle folding chair to the fabric on her table to the wisteria overhead.
LEFT: Hybrid tea roses draw the eye into the garden.

drawn from nature 111

THYME BEGAN IN A GARDEN

LEFT: Greenery cascades right over the tops of the windows and into the living room. Birdcages, floral cushions, and rugs patterned with abstract botanicals carry the theme throughout. *ABOVE, OPPOSITE TOP, AND OPPOSITE BOTTOM LEFT:* "A good designer should lead your eye from one focal point to the next," says Karen. Birdhouses, baskets, chairs both large and child-size, tin-can men, sculptures, and aviaries ensure there's never a dull visual moment. *OPPOSITE BOTTOM RIGHT:* Karen keeps her flower arrangements and garden reading together on trays for portable pleasures that move easily from indoors to out.

of the outdoors as one big bolt of fabric unrolled, so that repeat groupings of the same plants appear every few feet—much as you'd use the same textile in different ways indoors, on the curtains at one end of the room and throw pillows on the other.

"It's important to bring nature in," says Karen. "It could be something so simple as acorns and chestnuts in fabulous crystal bowls or bittersweet ambling on armoires. You could put a birdbath in the entry hall and fill it with African violets and orchids. Instead of cut flowers, whole growing plants in cachepots are more economical. An antique shovel could become a curtain rod, or an upside-down rake could hold keys—and on and on." At the same time, she doesn't hesitate to bring the indoors out, with chairs, tables, and garden structures peeking out among plants.

Karen also paints outsize images. For instance, a nine-foot-long sunflower canvas decorates a wall of her bedroom. "I feel like Pollyanna in the morning. It's impossible to not be cheerful when you fill your home with images like these."

TERRAIN tip

To unite spaces like patios with the indoors, paint fences and decks a watered-down shade of your interior color.

BELOW: Though it looks like part of some grand design, this mini-cottage was thrown together from plywood. Its six French doors were fortuitously waiting in the wings for their moment in the sun. With pots placed invitingly outside, it becomes a satellite room of the main house.

ABOVE: Seatless chairs were originally slated to get wire-mesh seats filled with "fairy gardens," but the more Karen looks at them, the more she likes their simplicity.

RIGHT: The 1880s paneling in Karen's "green room" is original. To play it up, she painted the walls yellow-green and the trim a barely-there celadon. The sofa slipcover is a similar shade. "Everything is in the same color family, though it doesn't match exactly."

the bare necessities

The haiku of furnishing schemes, spare spaces let every object stand
up and be counted. Not just for bachelors and recent college graduates, the lean
look appeals to the organized, neat-as-a-pin soul in all of us. Just a few
well-chosen pieces are all you need.

CHAPTER FIVE

SOONER OR LATER, WE ALL HAVE THE URGE TO scale back. Think of a light-drenched artist's loft with soaring ceilings, furnished with just an easel and a chair, and you get an inkling of the allure of spare. By editing our possessions, we create a *pied-à-terre* for creativity, a place that allows growth without constraint. If you have a lot going on in your life, maybe you want—you need—your home to be a peaceful haven.

Fortunately, there are many ways to cut clutter and eliminate excess. A furniture avant-garde has existed for at least one hundred years with this precise purpose in mind, experimenting with new ideas, new materials, and new forms. Why not reap the benefit of their ideas?

For instance, there's the Arts and Crafts movement, which became a potent force at the turn of the 20th century. It condemned excessive living spaces and overdone ornament; its simple oak furniture is perfect even now in a minimalist environment.

In 1915, the French architect Le Corbusier declared "*L'Esprit Nouveau*"—the new spirit. At the international exhibition he built a small house with a quietly classical interior. It was furnished with just a few select pieces of decidedly modern design as well as overscale paintings. The house was definitely before its time—and prompted an aesthetic revolution. During the interwar years that followed, designers stripped down their work and attempted to use as few components as possible in their creations—for instance, a chair made of a single piece of bent plywood—not only to encourage aesthetic purity but also to facilitate mechanized production.

The modernist ideal of simple, flat surfaces and basic forms, of rooms with minimal decoration, was gradually entering the public arena. Early contemporary houses of the 1930s were built with open plans, which at the time seemed revolutionary. Today, it's a trend again to build wall-free living spaces, and the pieces from that era still look right at home. The designs are so classic that many are still in production. You'll know

OPPOSITE: **A spare Arts and Crafts settee works beautifully with contemporary art and a geometric-patterned carpet.** *TOP:* **The secret of minimalism is the invisible force fields between a few well-chosen objects. There's a creative tension between the cast-iron dog doorstop and a mottled walnut chair.** *ABOVE:* **In the same way, a steel tripod table and enclosed banister echo the grid of a wall-hung rack.**

the bare necessities   119

them when you see them, from Mies van der Rohe's cantilevered chrome-plated tubular steel chairs of 1931, available with leather or cane seats, to Le Corbusier's *Le Grand Confort* leather-and-steel armchair of 1928, any of which look like they might have been designed yesterday.

Modern furniture from the mid-century is equally in keeping with the clean-line look. Charles Eames designed a skinny sofa whose back actually folded down. Chairs and tables became more sculptural and organic, taking free-form amoeba, flying-saucer, and butterfly shapes. The Atom clock—metal supports with brightly colored ball feet, cocktail-cherry style—marked time in everyone's kitchen. Three-legged kidney-shaped tables seemed to float in air. There's a thread of connectedness that runs through these mid-century pieces. Most ardent collectors mix them all, and create fairly purist environments. Those of us who are still merely infatuated with the period often flirt with one piece, then add another, and finally fall in love.

OPPOSITE: **In orderly facing rows, Le Corbusier's *Grand Confort* armchairs have a tranquil presence in a living room.** *BELOW LEFT:* **To keep her interiors simple and streamlined, one designer accessorizes with her collection of sculpted metal compacts from the 20th century.** *BELOW RIGHT:* **At first glance, you might think this tall-backed couch came out of the 1930s, from its leather arms and seat and its metal base. But the playful fabric treatment along its back reveals that it's pure 1950s. Twenty years ago, you probably couldn't have given it away. Nowadays, collectors go on cross-country pilgrimages in search of pieces like this.**

Glass and metal objects work beautifully in simple interiors because of their light-reflective qualities.

BRILLIANT tip

Entering this dining room, a painting by Belinda Lee is the first thing the eye sees. The concept of outsize art being a room's dominant furnishing—and its most colorful—is one of Modernism's earliest innovations. The glass-topped table and pale maple Queen Anne-style chairs set on a cream Berber rug enhance the airiness of the space.

IN THE WORDS OF WILLIAM MORRIS, THE BRITISH FOUNDER of the Arts and Crafts movement, "Have nothing in your house that you do not know to be useful or believe to be beautiful."

With this pearl of wisdom in mind, cast a cold eye on your surroundings. How attached are you really to that pullout sofa bed from your first apartment? The cat-scratched pink slipper chair covered with coffee stains? The television caddy you no longer use? They were good while they lasted, but maybe it's time to move on.

Keep only the things that are most meaningful to you. Build your decor around that one special piece. Perhaps a Biedermeier settee with charcoal pinstripe upholstery. An outsize painting. Or plush cocoa-colored French club chairs from the 1920s. Understatement is key.

GETTING THAT LOOK:

PEARLY FRAMES

Family pictures needn't be framed in heavy silver or gold in a crowded gallery. Try our lighter version instead.

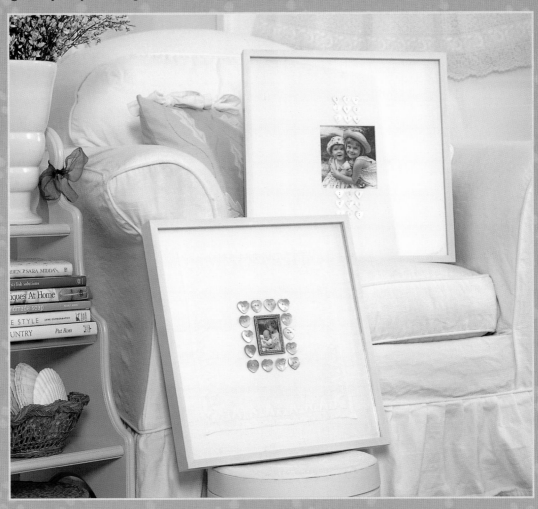

How to make 'em:

1. CUT WHITE MAT BOARD with a utility knife to fit a pale wood frame (or have the frame shop do it), with an interior window to fit the photograph. With the mat board as a template, trace a window in the center of a white handkerchief, using a seamstress pencil. Snip out the window from the material.

2. SEW MOTHER-OF-PEARL buttons in a pattern of your choice surrounding the window.

3. ATTACH THE PHOTOGRAPH to the back of the mat board with archival-quality glue stick.

4. ATTACH THE HANDKERCHIEF to the mat board with spray mount. Assemble all the materials in the frame.

Optional: For a bit of glitter, use a dimestore frame or rhinestone shoe buckle to frame the window surrounding the photograph.

OPPOSITE: Designer Molly Leach created a corner that allows the eye to rest on two key spots; first, on a whimsical framed artwork whose lively geometrics require only a simple frame; second, on a chair where a sunset orange throw meets its match in a leather briefcase. *ABOVE:* In HOME COMPANION editor Barbara Martin's home office, understated kiwi painted walls become the canvas for displays that include an old tractor steering wheel, pocket watches, and enamel wall numbers from France. *RIGHT:* Centered precisely over a carved wood bench, a panoramic senior class photo pleasingly echoes its boxy shape.

LEFT: When we hear the words "Hollywood glamour," the sleek movie sets of the 1930s and 1940s come to mind, where Myrna Loy and William Powell might feel at home having cocktails. It's all reinterpreted in one St. Louis home in a low–key way, with sensuous curves, elegant lines, and silver accessories.

ABOVE: In a cluttered environment, none of these antique boxes would make much of an impression. Yet arranged sparely on glass shelves, they seem to float in air, allowing onlookers to admire each detail.

BELOW: Metal, glass, and laminate— "materials of the future"—are warmed by maple panels in a home office. Historically speaking, the L-shaped desk arrangement is known as the action office, a term coined in the late 1960s to describe a setup that allows employees to hide "meaningful clutter."

LEFT: While the stainless steel counter-tops, stools, appliances, and work island create a clean, futuristic look, pale birch cabinets and green McCoy pottery warm up the room. *OPPOSITE TOP:* Iron bases on rattan stools keep this cream-colored kitchen from seeming to float away. Though contemporary, the stools completely embody the early-20th-century design vision of chair as "sitting object"—that is, a sculptural yet functional object. *OPPOSITE BOTTOM LEFT:* On its own, a solid black table could be a tad too monolithic. But paired with old-fashioned wooden chairs, it invites you to gather round. Black in the lampshade and in the grouting of the granite fireplace in a pale scheme adds graphic punch. *OPPOSITE BOTTOM RIGHT:* A Baby Ben alarm clock plays off brushed nickel faucets in a serene still life.

METAL'S FIRST GREAT DECORATING MOMENT CAME IN 1925, when Marcel Breuer designed the "Wassily" chair, named after artist Wassily Kandinsky, who commissioned it. The chair consisted of a tubular steel frame with slingback seats and arms of leather or canvas. (Before that, metal furniture had been reserved for commercial buildings.) Other designers ran with the idea, and the public bought it. Aluminum, which had been used for machinery, now entered the home for kitchen and giftware. Monel metal, a copper-nickel alloy that was a precursor to stainless steel, became popular for domestic sinks and cabinets. Chrome-plated coffee and tea services in simple geometric forms also appeared.

Metal's popularity soared. Soon even Emily Post was singing its praises, writing that never had there been "so complete an answer to the housewife's prayer—appealing not only to the eye, but to practical requirements." What more could a housewife ask for in her home?

METALLIC tip *From stainless steel to silver, all metals go together, whatever their origin.*

LEFT: When you choose a tactile mix of fabrics and furnishings, it makes the most modern space seem rich. Instead of color, textures give a sunroom its interest. The weave of a rattan sofa, the clean lines of redwood flooring, and the crispness of a bamboo centerpiece all invite bare hand (and foot) inspection. Like a rock in a landscape, the brushed steel coffee table seems to keep it all from wandering off into the trees. The one bright note of color, from a tangerine-hued throw pillow, gives the eye a place to rest.

ABOVE: In a minimalist lifestyle, resist the urge to pile too many elements into a vignette. Remember that each object takes on greater importance when it has a little breathing space. Still, everyone likes a little variety, so satisfy that urge by rotating displays to suit the seasons. Here snapdragons and gladiolus in a galvanized metal vase contrast with the smooth, hard river stones.

WHEN YOU COME HOME FROM A BUSY DAY AT THE OFFICE, the last thing you need is visual information overload. Choose just a few colors for the overall scheme. You could do a whole house in a series of minutely varied off whites—linen, snow, seashell, orchid—and never get bored. The space becomes an open, modern canvas where art—and people—can shine.

But it doesn't necessarily have to be white. Pale green. Sunwashed lemon. Dove gray. Blush. These almost-neutrals seem to dissolve into air. Let a pale spectrum envelop the entire house. Create small harmonies, quiet repetitions of patterns and colors that only your subconscious will recognize.

Slipcover the furniture in a coarse indigo linen. Cover the floor with sisal rugs. Search out bamboo or rattan tables, old clocks whose faces have turned sepia, creamy plates and jugs. Use a panel of seagrass for a headboard.

It's easy to find those small pale touches, but how do you furnish several rooms in a consistently pale look? The simple answer is Scandinavian Modern. The famous Finnish designer and architect Alvar Aalto declared wood "deeply human." He bent plywood into a single piece to form his contoured plywood chairs and started the "blond look" revolution.

Characterized by elegant simplicity, these pieces continue to be made today. Which is not to say that only the Scandinavians used pale wood effectively. The Heywood Wakefield Company and Russel Wright (with his American Moderne line) both produced exemplary wood furniture that continues to enjoy a tremendous renaissance into the 21st century.

OPPOSITE: **All-beige interiors are nurturing and soothing. Blond wood provides a restful composition in a bedroom.**
ABOVE: **Decorating with a few objects—like the silver on the mantel— "fills out" the room while keeping it light.**

Mary's Penchant for Snazz

"A design guru called beige perfect in a pale color scheme. Sounds boring to me! Give me sherbet hues—oranges and lilacs. They all mix easily with white."

In Mary's sitting room, soft also means sophisticated. Though in its original form, Arts and Crafts furniture was never white, a contemporary interpretation fulfills the minimalist's criterion for simplicity while also keeping the palette pale.

BELOW: Classic beadboard paneling that reaches straight to the ceiling gives a feeling of light and space in a Chicago bath. The glass-brick window conjures houses of the 1930s, which often featured great expanses of this material in place of opaque walls. An open-weave towel basket is an easy way to bring line and pattern to the room while retaining its open feel. ABOVE: Though durable, metal always gives rooms a slightly luxe feeling, as with a stainless steel sink and the silver accessories that complement it. RIGHT: In the same room, more silver gleams at tubside. Photos from the past century mimic the simple geometry of the windows. For the tub's deep surround and paneled front, the owner avoided more imposing materials and chose maple and limestone, which keep the palette pale.

AN ARTFUL LIFE:

Julie &
David Walker

She's an art director. He's an artist who works at home, drawing inspiration from everything around him. So maybe you'd expect their St. Louis home to be filled to the rafters with stuff. Instead, in the belief that creativity comes from an open mind, Julie and David Walker make the most of the minimum.

Their 1935 center hall colonial is a hybrid of sorts: very traditional in looks but small enough to be cottagey. Since they'd moved from a larger house to this one, the Walkers needed to make some big decisions about how to deal with the space cutback—while planning for a baby on the way.

Because the house makes up for its size with overscale details like a grand living room fireplace and stunning bay windows, they resolved to make the most of these features: there would be no wallpaper, no heavy-duty window treatments, and a consistently light palette of what Julie calls "warm, cozy neutrals." This meant lots

FAR LEFT: Julie's secret weapon for clutter control—baskets everywhere. *LEFT:* A single oversize teacup brought back from England makes a powerful visual statement in a niche at the top of a staircase.

the bare necessities   137

LEFT: Only sentimental objects win a place in the Walker home—inkwells that were a present to Julie from David sit on a desk made by her grandfather and presented to her for her tenth birthday.

OPPOSITE TOP: Rather than buying new dining room chairs, Julie unified disparate pieces of furniture with slipcovers. Not only do the green button-back designs hide flaws, but they also maintain an overall sense of order. Note the backdrop of barely-there diamonds painted in a pale shade of green, the color of tranquility. OPPOSITE BOTTOM LEFT: "We like to have our artwork and objects star," says Julie. A portrait by one of David's favorite contemporary artists, Skip Liepke, was a surprise gift from Julie.

OPPOSITE BOTTOM RIGHT: David's muted oil study of peonies captures the tranquil mood of his own home studio.

of "Lancaster Whitewash" from Benjamin Moore, which Julie says "has a slight green cast to it, depending on the light. Green is a great accent color."

They furnished the house with a spartan eye, relying on just a few comfortable pieces in each room. Instead of crowding tabletops with knickknacks, the Walkers shadow-box-framed small treasured objects and displayed them on the wall.

The Walkers have moved yet again, this time to a bigger house to make even more room for their two young daughters. At their new home, you'll find more baskets than before, in every room, keeping toys at bay, clothes at hand, newspapers and magazines tidy. But the Walkers have left their bulkier furniture behind—most notably the dining room set and the living room sofa. The same white hue as before covers the walls, though you'll notice a lot more chocolate browns and rich greens in the mix, the better to camouflage handprints of growing girls. "We're going for serene," says Julie. "And sometimes that means you have to shift your palette a bit."

PAINTERLY tip

When you keep the palette neutral and the furnishings minimal, even tiny details stand out.

the bare necessities

BELOW: "We like showing off little things, which stop and make you look," says David of the small treasures which the couple hang on doors. Here, clockwise from top left, a Victorian calling card holder; an heirloom pocket watch; old-fashioned eye-glasses that Julie's grandmother bought for her at a tag sale in her old hometown; and a dust broom that once belonged to a favorite great-aunt.
ABOVE: Orderly, symmetrical groupings are the key to a restful home, believe the Walkers. Even the flowerpots are arranged in graphic style. RIGHT: Bleached maple cabinets and recessed lighting do much to expand the visual boundaries of the kitchen. The three-sided table forms an abbreviated breakfast nook.

credits

So many wonderful, creative people have brought us into their homes to inspire us. I would like to thank them all from the bottom of my heart. Mary

PHOTOGRAPHY ON PAGES 61 (LEFT), 69 BY GORDON BEALL; PAGE 36 BY CATHERINE BOGERT; PAGES 72, 119 (BOTTOM) BY JIM HEDRICH; PAGES 98, 131 BY BILL HOLT; PAGES 48 (RIGHT), 63 BY MIKE JENSEN; PAGE 106 (TOP) BY ERIC JOHNSON; PAGES 10, 120 BY JENIFER JORDAN; PAGE 127 (BOTTOM) BY MARK LOHMAN; PAGES 18-19 BY BOB MAUER; PAGES 41, 75 BY MATTHEW MILLMAN; PAGE 95 (BOTTOM LEFT) BY BRAD SIMMONS; PAGES 2, 50 (LEFT), 51, 92 (TOP), 93 BY JUDITH WATTS; ALL OTHER PHOTOGRAPHY BY BARBARA ELLIOTT MARTIN.

65	HOMEOWNERS: Roberta and David Williamson, Berea, Ohio
66	HOMEOWNER: Julie Kelston, Nyack, New York
67	HOMEOWNER: Ted Frankel, Chicago, Illinois
68	HOMEOWNER: Bianca Juarez, Los Angeles, California
69	HOMEOWNER: Sharne Algotsson, Philadelphia, Pennsylvania
70-71	STUDIO OWNER: Lane Smith, New York, New York
72	HOMEOWNER: Esther Fishman, Chicago, Illinois
73	top: DESIGNER: Cissie Cooper, Los Angeles, California
	bottom left: HOMEOWNER: Jennifer Myers, Austin, Texas
	bottom right: HOMEOWNER: Jeanine Anderson Guncheon, Oak Park, Illinois
74	HOMEOWNER: Jeanine Anderson Guncheon, Oak Park, Illinois
75	RADIO FLYER TRICYCLE from Treasure Island Flea Market, San Francisco, California
76	HOMEOWNERS: Belinda and Jesika Hare, Fredericksburg, Texas
77	HOMEOWNER: Jeff Jones, Atlanta, Georgia
78-79	HOMEOWNER: Mary Engelbreit, St. Louis, Missouri
80	HOMEOWNER: Martha Young, Peaks Island, Maine
81	top: HOMEOWNERS: Jeff and Anne O'Connor, Oak Park, Illinois
	bottom: HOMEOWNERS: John and Tracy Porter, Princeton, Wisconsin
82-87	HOMEOWNERS: Belinda and Jesika Hare, Fredericksburg, Texas
88	"FRUCHIE" LAMPSHADE, "ANDUZE" GREEN URNS, "LA FLEUR" PLATE, "JERPONT" GOBLET from Pierre Deux, Nanuet, New York. ITALIAN TERRA-COTTA SAUCERS from Nicholson Hardie, Dallas, Texas. RECTANGULAR FLOWER BASKET, VINTAGE WATERING CAN from Room Service, Dallas, Texas
89	left: HOMEOWNER: Sandy Koepke, Topanga Canyon, California
	right: HOMEOWNER: Jill Schwartz and Ron Ronan, Great Barrington, Massachusetts
90	HOMEOWNER: Frank Windler, St. Louis, Missouri
91	HOMEOWNER: Ruth Touhill, Dutzow, Missouri
92	top: HOMEOWNERS: Roberta and David Williamson, Berea, Ohio
	bottom: HOMEOWNERS: Belinda and Jesika Hare, Fredericksburg, Texas
93	HOMEOWNERS: Roberta and David Williamson, Berea, Ohio
94	HOMEOWNER: Dominique Pfahl, San Francisco, California
95	top: DESIGNER: Cissie Cooper, Los Angeles, California
	bottom right: HOMEOWNER: Pat Collier, Atlanta, Georgia
	bottom left: DESIGNER: Cissie Cooper, Los Angeles, California
96	HOMEOWNER: Anne McCoole, St. Louis, Missouri
97	HOMEOWNERS: Kim and Joseph Morrow, Alton, Illinois
98	HOMEOWNERS: Ron and Barbara Kiker, Spokane, Washington
99	HOMEOWNERS: Bill and Marie Trader, Chicago, Illinois
100	HOMEOWNER: Mary Engelbreit, St. Louis, Missouri
101	top right: HOMEOWNER: Mary Engelbreit, St. Louis, Missouri
	bottom left: HOMEOWNER: Marcy Spanogle, St. Louis, Missouri
102	HOMEOWNER: Sheila Griesedieck, St. Louis, Missouri
103	left: HOMEOWNERS: John and Tracy Porter, Princeton, Wisconsin
	right: HOMEOWNERS: Tom and Mary Ott, St. Louis, Missouri
104-105	DESIGNERS: Suzedie Clement and Laura Miller of Brazwell & Ballantine Ltd., St. Louis, Missouri
106	top: HOMEOWNER: Susan Smith, St. Louis, Missouri
	bottom: HOMEOWNER: Sonja Willman, Clayton, Missouri
107	HOMEOWNER: Suzedie Clement, St. Louis, Missouri
108	top: HOMEOWNER: Marcy Spanogle, St. Louis, Missouri
	bottom: HOMEOWNER: Candy Rosen, Laguna Beach, California
109	HOMEOWNER: Cissie Cooper, Los Angeles, California
110-115	HOMEOWNER: Karen Dominguez-Brann, Santa Monica, California
116	HOMEOWNERS: Martha Young and Jock McQuilkin, Atlanta, Georgia
117	left: HOMEOWNER: Paul Cavalli, St. Louis, Missouri
	right: HOMEOWNER: Rose Hicks, Fredericksburg, Texas
118	HOMEOWNER: Julie Kelston, Nyack, New York
119	top: HOMEOWNER: Paul Cavalli, St. Louis, Missouri
	bottom: HOMEOWNER: Esther Fishman, Chicago, Illinois
120	HOMEOWNER: Nancy Rosenbaum, Chicago, Illinois
121	HOMEOWNERS: Karen and Stuart Johnson, St. Louis, Missouri
122	HOMEOWNER: Paul Cavalli, St. Louis, Missouri
123	DESIGNER: Julie Walker, St. Louis, Missouri
124	HOMEOWNERS: Lane Smith and Molly Leach, New York, New York
125	top: HOMEOWNER: Barbara Elliott Martin, St. Louis, Missouri
	bottom: HOMEOWNERS: Rod and Jill Perth, San Marino, California
126	HOMEOWNER: Paul Cavalli, St. Louis, Missouri
127	top: HOMEOWNER: Paul Cavalli, St. Louis, Missouri
128	HOMEOWNERS: Carol and Terry Crouppen, St. Louis, Missouri
129	top: HOMEOWNERS: Martha Young and Jock McQuilkin, Atlanta, Georgia
	bottom left: HOMEOWNER: Paul Cavalli, St. Louis, Missouri
	bottom right: HOMEOWNERS: Hugh Sollo and Allan Smessaert, Kankakee, Illinois
130	HOMEOWNER: Peggy Lipton, St. Louis, Missouri
131	HOMEOWNER: Lorene Edwards Forkner, Seattle, Washington
132	HOMEOWNER: Paul Cavalli, St. Louis, Missouri
133	right: HOMEOWNER: Mary Engelbreit, St. Louis, Missouri
	left: HOMEOWNER: Paul Cavalli, St. Louis, Missouri
134	top: HOMEOWNER: Paul Cavalli, St. Louis, Missouri
	bottom: HOMEOWNERS: Jeff and Anne O'Connor, Oak Park, Illinois
135	HOMEOWNER: Paul Cavalli, St. Louis, Missouri
136-141	HOMEOWNERS: Julie and David Walker, St. Louis, Missouri
144	HOMEOWNER: Dominique Pfahl, San Francisco, California

To join us as a subscriber to MARY ENGELBREIT'S HOME COMPANION magazine, please call us toll-free: (800) 826-3382.